Don't just Tithe-Plan Save and Invest$$

By Daniel Magee

Daniel Magee is a Houston based executive pastor who has serviced the insurance and mortgage industry for 20 years. He also serves as treasurer for the non-profit organization named a humble seed foundation His books combine both the wisdom of the industry and the word of God to help people discover their untapped potential. He is married to Kathy Magee and the two have multiple children. Born and raised in southern Mississippi, he is determined to use his knowledge and gifts to bring positive change to the life of every reader.

Let me start this book by giving glory to God for helping me complete this project. I also am very thankful for the love and support of my beautiful wife Kathy Magee. You are amazing honey. This is dedicated to you, our children and all of the wonderful people who are a part of our lives.

Introduction

Have you ever wondered if the believer was created to do and experience so much more. After a lifetime of being taught the importance of kingdom giving, there are some that have never been given tools to intentionally create a better life for themselves and their families. This book endeavors to discover the necessary financial principles that can place the faithful kingdom giver in a place of Sufficient Provision. It is with great joy and humility that I present to you this subject:

Don't just Tithe-Plan, Save and Invest

Table of Contents

1) The Things We Were Taught
2) When Hope Meets Faith
3) Sufficient Provision
4) You are Destined to Reign
5) The What if Factor
6) Write the Vision
7) Passing the Torch
8) Where Do We Go From Here?

Preface

The world we live in today is quite different than the one of our ancestors . When it comes to biblical instruction and training that has been passed down, this generation does not accept truths until they have applied and tried it for themselves. Many biblical teachings have recently come up in controversy in the modern church media. One of those, happens to be tithing. This book does not in any way seek to question a basic principle of the word. It begins and flows with the understanding that scripture gives us healthy boundaries and a platform from which to live our lives. From this place we can discover the abundant path to which each of us is called.

I was sitting in my living room enjoying a good Saturday evening read by a man named Ramit Sethi. Ramit happens to be an iconic financial guru who helps people discover their rich life based on the things they enjoy and appreciate the most. He works with multiple clients, teaching them how to shore up their financial lives and get the most out of their time with family. Somewhere in the midst of my reading, the thought occurred to me, We need more teaching on Kingdom faith and finances in the church. It would assist the people of God in maximizing their gifts, resources and potential.

The enemy has propagated a lie that being financially sound is not biblical. But we know better.

The Idea that God wants us to struggle does not line up with scripture. From the day God created the earth, he placed gold and other resources in the ground and instructed his son Adam to properly steward (take dominion over) over the earth. From the very beginning, God commanded Adam to be fruitful and multiply.

We also continue to see in the scriptures, God attaches blessing and increase to those who are faithful and obedient .

In light of this fact, I have written this book concerning Kingdom faith and finances and I pray that it is a blessing unto each of you.

By the time you finish it, you will see the value of investing in your children, your marriage, your personal development and financial assets. The results will payoff a thousand times over. It is definitely time for the church to move from the season of manna in the wilderness to effective management in the promised land.

1 The Things we were Taught

As long as I can remember, the church community with whom My family was connected can be described as faithful believers. We taught the principles of the bible such as salvation, sanctification, justification, faith and kingdom giving. Kingdom giving was often addressed in the form of tithes and offerings. In the book of Malachi 3:10 the Lord says," Bring the tithe (tenth) of your increase in to my store house and prove me if I will not open up the windows of heaven and pour you out a blessing that you will not have room to receive." We taught that God loves a cheerful giver. We were right. After all life is a stewardship. We were created by Him to fulfill our living assignments and one day stand before him to hear the words, "Well done good and faithful servant."

In addition to that, we were taught that the word of God says, "My God shall supply all of your needs according to His riches in Glory by Christ Jesus (philippians 4:19). As a preacher's kid I believed every word of it. It was truth and it therefore holds the power to set us free. I even grew up to preach those same truths to the congregation that I led and fellowshipped with.

What can be more comforting than to know that if God is for us, it matters not who is against us. The whole counsel of the bible says that God the Creator loves us and wants to have intimate fellowship with his creation. You see, from the beginning, God had a magnificent plan for you and I that he has never let go of. You can find it in the book of Genesis. After God made the heavens and the earth, he looked at everything and declared that it was good. And then, God created the apex of his earthly creation when he says, "Let us make man in our own image. Let him have dominion over the earth and the sea and every creeping, swimming, and flying thing." Yes friends, God had grand thoughts about who you are and what you are capable of. When he made man, he then said that his creation is very good.

If you are a human being, then you have this special ability to become much more than you appear to be. Your assignment is to be fruitful and multiply. In doing this, you will take dominion over the earth. Now, you can't rule over the whole earth by yourself. But there are areas of influence, skills and gifting that you are called to discover and optimize in your life. That means that you are the original transformer. There is more to you than meets the eye. If you are to truly become all that the Father has destined, you must be willing to learn and always be growing. If you stay teachable, your value will continue to increase. To that end, this book is written to show you that the Father's good plan for you is still on the table waiting for you to possess it. Now, let's take a journey to discover the missing link between where we are at and where we are called to arrive.

2 When Hope meets Faith

Anyone who has ever preached the gospel can tell you that it is the good news. Good news to the bound, good news to the sick, the broke and the oppressed. It all culminates in the story of a father who would go to great extents to restore his lost children. He knows exactly what good plans he has in store for them. He was even willing to sacrifice His son so that many sons could be restored. That one son, friends, is the anointed one. Discovering the power that is in his name will set you on the journey of a lifetime.

As I look back on my experience of proclaiming the gospel, I can see that it was hope that we gave to each parishioner. Hope helps those in despair to believe God for a miracle. We preach hope which produces faith in the God who can heal our sickness, restore our families, protect our lives, and save our souls. The bible says, faith comes by hearing. And hearing comes through the Word. We have preached hope on every the corner of the earth and the world would do with it whatever they would. God has remained faithful to His promises throughout the years.

While the principles we preached showed men the way to eternal life, that is not the main focus of the book you are reading. I decided to write this book because in many parishioners' lives, hope was all they had. Faith would keep the lights on, the roof over their heads, and clothes on their backs. Because, after all, God cares for His people.

However, I can't help but consider that maybe something was missing in our Sunday morning messages. Maybe there was something that could help empower our parishioners to live at their fullest potential. Don't blame me, I'm a pastor. My calling is to desire the well being of the people. They had the faith. What they needed was tools and understanding to live on a higher financial platform. With that revelation, I realized that financial literacy should be taught in schools and the church as well. Precious time and resources are wasted when everyone is left to figure things out along the way.

When we had nothing else, we always had God, who is more than enough in every generation.

I loved seeing God work a miracle in the lives of His people. The only reason I am here today is because of a lifetime of being protected by the miraculous hand of God. However, I was recently moved to consider that in the area of resources, there is something better than a miracle. Believe me, I know just what you are thinking, Blasphemy!!

What could be better than a miracle? The manifestation of the supernatural assures and reminds us that God will never leave us nor forsake us. Evangelist Oral Roberts used to say," A miracle is either coming towards you or moving past you at every given moment." When people did not have abundant resources and opportunities for whatever reason, they had hope. They walked in faith and love. They took a little and made it stretch to feed a whole community. Watching God's people come to the alter as we stood in faith and agreement with them for results was always exhilarating when the results came back. One thing that I can say is, God is faithful.

Let's be honest. We have all needed a miracle at some time in our lives. Remember that time when you called out to God and he answered your prayer. I remember on so many occasions.

So I ask you," What could be better than a miracle?"

I dare clear my throat when I answer you. Are you ready? Sufficient Provision!!

3 Sufficient Provision

To be in position where there is no worry as to how the bills will be paid. That is, say it with me now, Sufficient Provision. It is being in a position where your child's college expense is set aside. The car replacement and repair, set aside. Retirement you say? Well on track. Guilt heavy spending is a thing of the past. The only type of spending you have now is guilt free. It is the place where you may not be a millionaire, but you have learned how to take control of your finances as opposed to hanging on for dear life. For some, wealth is the only experience that they have known since childhood. It was both demonstrated and passed down to the next generation.

For others, it's an unfamiliar experience. The starting line is not at the same place. All of their lives, they had to fight. It was enough just to hold on to Gods unchanging hand while fighting for economic survival. While they did not have much, they put the education and well being of their kids first. They sacrificed their present situation to insure their kids futures. To them I say well done and bravo.

You see, there are people who can judge those that have a lesser credit score. But the truth is somewhat deeper than what meets the eye. While one kid was being groomed for Harvard the other was working odd end jobs to help mom pay for simple family necessities. If you think the playing field is even and everyone has the same opportunity then you should look a little deeper. But that's another book for another day, however. Today's power word is, drum roll please....", Sufficient Provision."

It is hidden right there in the scriptures and we sometimes just stumble over it.

John 10:10

10 The thief cometh not, but for to steal, and to kill, and to destroy: I have come that they might have life, and that they might have it more abundantly.

Our adversary has had one agenda from day one. To bring loss and destruction to mankind. He started with Adam and wants to continue with you. God our Father, sent Jesus to make available to us a better life. An abundant life that keeps on flowing higher and higher into the perfect will of God. God did not design a beggarly life for you.

3 John 2 says Beloved, I wish above all things that you would prosper and be in health even as your soul prospers.

That tells us that there is something that must happen on the inside (our mind, will and emotions) that will affect what happens on the outside. The prosperous soul is the one who knows first of all, that they are loved of the Father. Secondly, they have been sent here with a purpose. Thirdly, heaven is standing to assist them in becoming fruitful in whatever area of gifting they are called to. So wave goodbye to the lies of the enemy that say you are destined to struggle. Set your eyes on the promises of God and begin to acquire the knowledge and tools that will help you possess your inheritance.

You will be surprised at what happens when you add knowledge and understanding to faith. You will inherit the blessing of Abraham. Which means you will be blessed to be a blessing to all nations.

4 You are Destined to Reign

Some people go around with their head hanging down because they feel that they were somehow forgotten by God. They haven't seen the abundant life that the scriptures speak of so it must not exist. My friend, nothing could be farther from the truth. God wants you to have your needs supplied so that you can live a fulfilling life. You were created to discover how great you can be. There is a purpose and destiny carved out in the mind of God with your name on it. In order to discover this purpose, you will need the necessary means to expand your mind with knowledge and wisdom. You will need access to continued education and secrets of the well entitled to open the door of opportunities to you and your family. You were not called live a small life but a grand one. How many lives were you created to improve and influence? How many of your innate abilities need to be cultivated to make the lives many others better?

David says it this way, " I will praise you Oh Lord for I am fearfully and wonderfully made." (Psalms 139:14)

The army asks you to be all that you can be. I am asking you to change the world for the glory of God and the good of humanity.

In order to do that, you will need a vision. You must also acquire wisdom and understanding. Scripture encourages us to get wisdom and understanding. You might also be surprised to find out that certain knowledge and understanding has been hidden from you. Or maybe you were just not ready to digest this information in your former years. No matter. There is a popular saying that goes this way, "When the student is ready, the teacher will show up."

When you come into the fullness of understanding who you are, you go from being a child in the house to being a Son/Daughter (ready and prepared to take on leadership of the family business).

Look at Galatians 4:1-2

1 What I am saying is that as long as an heir is underage, he is no different from a servant, although he owns the whole estate.

2 The heir is subject to guardians and trustees until the time set by his father.

Your appointed has come to be the head and not the tail. After Joseph was tested through trials, then his purpose of favor became clear. He was called to rule and rule well.

So it is with you and I. Life gives us a series of test that ultimately shape, sharpen and mature us. Once we have grown up through the process. We find that every experience prepared for a future responsibility. You see, the refining fire is that which brings forth pure gold.

5 The What if Factor

I don't always like to question things that happen in life. I rarely join in the game of what ifs. But today, let's play what If.

-What if keeping up with the Jones is keeping us from maximizing our financial goals?

One pastor I know once said, " We spend money that we don't have to buy things that we don't need in an effort to impress people that we don't like. I don't know about the like part but he was definitely on to something. Did you know that the lower income population are the ones who make up the biggest consumer market. The funds that should be going into savings and investments are going into a new pair of Nike shoes or a Mercedes for which we will struggle to keep up the maintenance. Now I am not against having nice things once we have determined that it fits our budget without straining our finances. How about spending that extra $600 in a business that can produce an income. Or maybe an investment that generates a passive income over time. That is not how the average person thinks. It is how the wealthy think. They use money to make money and purchase assets that will generate new income. By doing this, the saying is perpetuated. The rich get richer.

While the lower income population is busy selling the limited resource of time for money, the rich purchase assets that make them money. They don't buy toys that decrease their accounts. They take the money they make from their assets to reinvest it in new businesses. They then purchase toys that increase their value.

-What if new skill sets could cause you to level up your financial status?

That's right. Our society tells us that once we get our degree, that it's okay to stop learning. We switch to entertaining ourselves. Hold up friend. Netflix is not going to pay you to watch their shows. Would you rather be watching the lives of others or figuring out how to most effectively live your best life. Entertainment can be dangerous if it keeps us from continuing to work on ourselves.

With the consistency of change in the modern work place. We need to always be learning new skillsets. The more we increase our knowledge, the more we naturally increase our pay scale. Some skills just have more monetary value than others. Schooling can be an option. However, learning a lucrative trade is just as good or better sometimes. Whichever path you choose, make sure that the return on investment is worth the time and loans that are required to pursue it. Society is not going to figure that part out for you.

-What if there where some who use your lack of understanding against you.?

(In all of your getting, get an understanding Proverbs 4:7) What if they could sell you a car for 25k and make 45k from you all because you only care about affording the monthly payments. Say it with me," Bamboozled." It may seem odd but it is true. A portion of society is unaware that those high interest rates due to lower credit scores can cost them additionally thousands of dollars. It is not enough for us to determine if we can afford the monthly payments. We must adjust to making sound financial purchases.

-What if sound financial principles could change your tumultuous financial waters into a calm cruise of living life on purpose?

There are people who listen to and read books by financial strategists which creates an atmosphere of financial literacy. Unfortunately, it is not taught in the school system. It is not taught in our public forums. So we must be intentional about acquiring financial wisdom and helping each family make better long-term financial plans and goals.

Here's another what if. What if we have championed steady employment to the point where we have no perspective on the need for entrepreneurship?

When we go to work faithfully we create wealth for our employers. However, starting our own businesses can create wealth for our family legacy. It can also provide employment in our communities. So it is a win/win. Do not look over the possibility of finding wealth in your own personal vision and gifting even as you remain faithful to your place of employment. The scriptures declare that a man's gift will make room for him.

Your gift is that which God gave you the natural ability to do. Your purpose is the voice inside that directs you to your destination. Your job is what they require you to do for a paycheck. Your gift, however, is what you were called to do. For every eight hours you spend on the job, you should spend at least two hours developing your personal gift and vision. Your job is your seed. Your vision is the promised harvest.

The day will come when you will be able to buy back your time to spend with your family if you plan, save and invest.

When I consider all of the what ifs, the question is, wouldn't you want to know? Wouldn't you want to be empowered? God forbid that I should rob you of the right to be ignorant. Neither should I hold back the small amount of knowledge that I have received thus far.

6 Write the Vision

Habakkuk 2:2 says-write the vision and make it plain. Proverbs 29:12 says -without a vision the people perish (paraphrased).

What is next for you? Where is your family going. Have you been left out to sea in danger of financial shipwreck?

It is time to decide. Who am I? Where do I want my family to go?

What is our potential and how can we get there. Life is too short to be drifting haphazardly. It is time to Plan for the house, the wedding, the graduation and the retirement. It will look something like this.

Ask yourself some money questions.

Who is getting more value out of my life than I am? The bank pays you 2% on the average savings account while you turn around and pay them 24% to use their credit card. They will kindly charge $35 for overdrafts, and a benevolent $40 for late payments. With friends like this, who needs enemies!

Could they be using the rule of 72 against you? It is the rule of compounding interest. It is a powerful multiplier. It works when your money earns interest. And then your interest earns interest. When it comes to Interest, you're either paying it or you're collecting it. This is how the rich get richer and the poor get poorer. Their money will double in three years. (72÷24=3) Your savings will double in 72 years. (72÷2=36). Funny how that works out.

Your time is not Money. You can accumulate more money but you cannot accumulate more time.

The average worker trades his time for money and thus can never get it back. The wealthy are smarter than this. They will pay you for your time while they are allowing their money to earn money. Here's a free tip. Your money Invested consistently in the right vehicle over a period of time will replace your job and retire you wealthy. You have a responsibility to your family to find the pathway of financial security.

 So write your plan. Determine if you need to increase your income or get rid of an unnecessary liability. Set your mind on buying or producing an asset that will bring you money while you sleep. If you can't afford one, create one through starting a business or writing a book. Pay off the credit card in full every month. Protect and improve your credit score by intention and focus. That one tip could save you thousands on yearly purchases. Level up and go live your abundant life.

Let's look at your current spending plan.

Ask yourself,

What is my income?

How much is the tithe 10%

How much is my debt 50%

How much am I saving 10%

How much am I investing 10%

How much is my free spending allotment 20%

Is your goal too high or is your income too low? Most people change the goal. Don't change the goal, change your income to keep you on track with meeting your goal. Add a skillset if you have to in order to generate additional income. Believe me, It will be worth it when you reach that projected target. No more mindless spending. From here on every expense has a monthly allocation. When you have mastered this. You will have greatly helped your financial woes. If you really want to be empowered, **Automate**!!

That's right. Set up automatic payments to each category of your budget and grow your net worth while you aren't even thinking about it. Imagine waking up 15 years later a half million dollars wealthier all because you put your financial affairs in order. It can be a reality if you are willing to Plan Save and Invest.

7 Passing the Torch

Once you have discovered your place of financial dominion teach your kids to teach their kids about acquiring and managing wealth with sound financial principles. Take the tools that the wealthy have always been privy to and empower your family to control their own destiny. It is important to establish a sound financial legacy upon which your family can stand. The bible says that, a good man/woman leaves an inheritance to their grandchildren.

That is how God thinks. He told Abraham that he would bless his seed in the earth. Our children should be standing on our shoulders as it relates to wealth acquisition. Once wealth is built up it grows much faster after starting slowly. That is why you can't afford for your family to start over in every generation. If you have not yet built up an inheritance, you can purchase an inheritance for your family in the form of life insurance. While there are many different kinds, the main point is to fill in the gap and position our posterity to win.

Once you have insured that there will be a family legacy, you must make sure that you teach your kids about how to handle money. Give them the tools and the lessons that you had to Learn the hard way because the information was not available to you. Give them the ability to not only work for gainful employment, but to plan to reign in this life. The bible says, "Train a child in the way that he should go. And when he is old, he will not depart from it." Proverbs 22:6

A lesson properly taught at a young age can empower a generation for a lifetime.

Give your kids accounts while they are growing and teach them how to handle money. There are so many kids who grow up with no handle on money because at home, money was never spoken of. Or, If it was spoken of, it was given a negative connotation. And yet, the word says if you are willing and obedient, you shall eat the good of the land.

If money were a bad thing why do we sacrifice time away from our family every day to attain it? If money were a bad thing, why would we be commanded to bring resources to the Lord's storehouse so that there would be a distributable provision.

There is one thing that some of God's dearest servants had in common. Do you remember Abraham, Job, Joseph and David? They controlled the finances of the market. Therefore they had influence. When they spoke, people listened. It was because of there command on the resources of society. It gave them influence and a platform to promote a kingdom world view. You see my friend, money is a tool that helps us fulfill our purpose. We don't love money but we must understand it's value as a means of trade currency in our society. We will not curse the next generation with ignorance but we shall empower them with wisdom and understanding.

8 Where do we go from Here?

This book is only the beginning of the change in mindset around money. The possibilities are endless once your focus is locked in. How you look at challenges will change. From now on, you will call a crisis an opportunity to solve a major problem. You will find that a new mindset automatically attracts new opportunities to plan save and invest. Your mind will conceive of ideas that will propel you towards wealth creation instead of frivolous consumption.

Quite possibly, you will be the next Joseph who will go on to save his people from starvation. It will definitely take resources. So declare these words, "Lord, I will be the one that you can use to feed a million people. Enlarge my understanding, and open my spiritual eyes to see the generational impact that I can have for my society. "

I decree that you will not be waiting for a miracle or a handout once you have grasped these principles. You will be the miracle hand that God can use to help the unhelpable and love the unlovable. You will teach the unteachable and reach the unreachable. By wisdom and understanding you will acquire the necessary influence to live at your fullest potential. The world will be the better because of it. Most of all, when the question arises surrounding the tithe in our generation, You will be able to tell them, "Don't just Tithe-Plan Save and Invest.

Now go out and live your purpose while achieving your dreams. If God is for you, who can be against you. God bless.